# VIOLA FLETCHER

**BEYOND A CENTURY, AN ENTHRALLING STORY OF VIOLA FORD FLETCHER, THE OLDEST SURVIVOR OF THE TULSA RACE MASSACRE**

LIZA MICHAEL

Copyright@2023

# LIZA MICHAEL

**ALL RIGHTS RESERVED**

# CONTENTS

1. **PREAMBLE**

2. **EARLY LIFE**
   Childhood
   Family Life and More

3. **TULSA RACE MASSACRE: THE DARK DAYS OF 1921**
   The Horrifying Nights
   A Call for Justice: Three Voices from Tulsa
   The Heartfelt Reminiscence

4. **VIOLA FLETCHER'S VOICE: A SOUND HOPE**

5. **THE VIOLA FORD FLETCHER FOUNDATION**

6. **VIOLA AND HUMANITY**
   VFFF Ghana
   About the Dzorwulu Special School
   About The New Horizon Special School
   About the Osu Children's Home

7. **FINAL THOUGHT**

# 1. PREAMBLE

Once upon a time, in Tulsa, Oklahoma, there was a wealthy neighborhood called Greenwood. It was in the middle of America's green fields. It was lovingly called "Black Wall Street," and its streets were full of people, money, and hopes for a better future. A young girl named Viola Ford Fletcher was one of the people who lived there.

On May 1, 1907, Viola was born on a sunny day, and her eyes were full of wonder and innocence. Little Viola's earliest memories should have been of happiness and the comfort of her home, where she lived with her family and four loved brothers. But in 1921, something terrible happened that turned her life upside down. Greenwood's bright days ended when Viola was only seven years old. One fateful night, as the stars twinkled, a group of angry people who didn't like people of different races came to the quiet neighborhood.

Viola was asleep in her warm bed when her mother's desperate words woke her up. She could tell that her mother was in a hurry as she quickly gathered her children and urged them to leave their safe place.

Outside, everything was falling apart. People screamed, homes burned down, and the once-bustling streets were full of fear and chaos. In the middle of the terrible chaos, the Fletcher family could only take the clothes on their backs and the memories of a home they had to leave because of violence.

Years turned into decades, and while the Greenwood neighborhood tried to heal, the scars of that night stayed, especially for Viola. Every time she closed her eyes, the night terrors came back: the piercing screams, the brutal violence of the white mob, the flames that seemed to reach the sky, and the heartbreaking sight of her community in ruins.

Her strength shone brightly in the face of life's problems, like a tree that gets bigger and stronger even in the worst weather. Love, family, and hard work are all important parts of Viola's story. In 1932, she promised to spend the rest of her life with Robert, and the two of them set out on a trip full of hopes and dreams. As World War II threw the world into chaos, the couple moved west to California, where they worked in factories and did their small part in the huge war effort.

But when the war ended and the world started to get back to normal, Viola and Robert followed their hearts and went back to their beloved Oklahoma. They raised their three children, two sons and a girl, in Bartlesville, which became their "cradle." Life had its ups and downs. While Viola carefully put together a warm home and cleaned for other people, Robert traveled the roads of Oklahoma, sometimes driving a truck and sometimes making sure a petrol station ran smoothly.

Even though the hands of the clock kept moving, Viola's strong will didn't change. Even though she was 85, she kept working, showing what it means to be dedicated and persistent. Today, Mother Fletcher lives in Bartlesville, where her age of 109 years and 120 days shows how strong she is.

Still, despite her age, Mother Fletcher knows the weight of despair, the chains of trauma, and the darkness that can cover minds. But her heart is full of hope, and she is sure that she can get through it. She once said in an elegant way that moving from hopelessness to hope is not easy, but that with grit and drive, anyone can enjoy life in all its glory.

At the age of 107, almost a hundred years later, Viola Fletcher became a symbol of strength and memory. On May 19, 2021, she went before the United States Congress. She did this with the strength that only survivors have. Hughes "Uncle Red" Van Ellis, who was 100 years old, was by her side. So was the strong Lessie Benningfield Randle, who had her own horrifying memories of that night. Their statement as a group was a plea for respect, justice, and compensation for a tragedy that had been forgotten for a long time.

Viola's voice was steady but full of pain as she talked about the terrible things she had seen. "I still see black guys getting shot and black bodies in the street. She said, with tears in her eyes, "I can still smell the smoke, hear the cries, and remember how bright the fire was." She painted a heartbreaking picture of a tragedy that hurt her so much that, even after all these years, she still finds comfort in sleeping upright on a couch with the lights on to keep the shadows of the past at bay.

Viola's statement wasn't just a personal story; it was a wake-up call. Her words matched the feelings of a group that wanted to be heard and given fair treatment. Viola Ford Fletcher's voice was heard all over the country, and she became known not only as a survivor but also as a symbol of hope. She made sure that the story of Greenwood and its lost Black Wall Street would never be forgotten again.

Viola's story is not about the hard times she went through but about her dream of a better world. Her dreams were bigger than her own happiness. Instead, they showed a bigger picture of a world where all children, no matter what their situation, had access to health, wealth, and knowledge. A world where pain, especially the pain of innocent children, was rare instead of common.

As we read the next parts, we'll be right there with Viola Fletcher. We will feel the difficulty of her problems and the joy of her time. We will see the start of The Viola Ford Fletcher Foundation, which will be a live reminder of how much she cared about helping people on the edges of society.

Get ready to be moved, and motivated, and to see a life that, even though it has been hard, shines brightly as a light of hope and determination. This is a fascinating story of Viola Fletcher's life, a journey of strength, vision, and love that never gives up.

## 2. EARLY LIFE

### *Childhood*

On May 10, 1914, Viola Ford Fletcher came into the world in the gentle hug of Comanche's rolling plains. She was born under the wide Oklahoma sky. This small town in southwestern Oklahoma, about 190 miles from the busy city of Tulsa, was where young Viola's story started.

She was the second oldest of John Wesley Ford and Lucinda Ellis Ford's eight children, and she was the shining gem in their crown. Viola had seven boys around, so her childhood was probably full of fun fights, laughs, and memories that would last her whole life. Her parents, who were strong and tough, worked as sharecroppers. They grew crops and ate what they grew. Their farm had fields of cotton that swayed in the wind, patches of corn that stood tall, and a mix of veggies that made a colorful picture.

Back then, life had its own special appeal. The Ford home was full of life, but it didn't have power or other modern conveniences. Instead, it was filled with a kindness that no technology could match. With stars in her eyes, little Viola held a rag doll she had made herself. It was her first friend, and it had been made with love and care.

But not all of Viola's memories from when she was young were happy. Just as she turned seven, a dark cloud started to gather over her world. A group of angry, hateful white people came to her mostly black neighborhood. The Fords had to leave the place they called home because of the scary screams, the burning fires, and the sound of the mob's footsteps. It was very hard to leave Tulsa, where hopes had turned into fears.

But the Ford spirit, which would not be broken, led them back to Tulsa in the end. The family came back, hanging on to hope and never giving up on the idea that home was where their hearts belonged.

During World War II, when the world was in chaos, young Fletcher went where only a few other women had gone before. As sparks flew and metal clanged, she stood shoulder to shoulder with experienced welders and helped them build huge ships that would sail on rough seas. This journey began when she got married to her handsome husband, Robert. Together, they went to the sunny coasts of California, where the factories never stopped working.

Under their big sky, Fletcher helped put down huge pieces of steel. Each piece added to the beauty of the ship that would go out on the water. She wasn't just a helper; she was part of a huge effort, like a cog in a machine that helped win the war.

## *Family Life and More*

When the war was over, Fletcher and Robert went back to the windy fields of Oklahoma hand in hand. As a safe place, they picked Bartlesville, a small town that sat next to Kansas. They raised three beautiful children here: two active boys and a beautiful girl.

Robert worked at a gas station, where the sound of truck engines and the smell of gas filled his days. Fletcher, on the other hand, found her balance in cleaning houses. Brick by brick, she built a life for her family with every sweep and scrub. She was so determined that even getting older couldn't slow her down. She worked until she was 85, which shows how strong-willed she was. But one day, after a short sigh of tiredness, she looked around and saw that she had made a safe place for herself. She no longer had to clean other people's homes and cars because she had her own.

In all these, her spirit was what really stood out, not what she had done. Racism, that dark cloud that was always around, never put out her light. To her, it was just a small whisper in the middle of her life's loud music.

Fletcher was a Black woman who was very proud of her race and history. In her eyes, she was just as much a person as anyone else. She breathed the same air, stayed true to her faith, and bled the same shade

of red as every other person on this planet.

## 3. TULSA RACE MASSACRE: THE DARK DAYS OF 1921

The Tulsa Race Massacre, which happened from May 31 to June 1, 1921, was one of the most violent acts against people of color in U.S. history. Several social and political issues led up to the killing, but the immediate cause was a fight between a young black guy and a young white lady.

On May 30, 1921, a 19-year-old Black shoe shiner named Dick Rowland went into a lift in the Drexel Building in Tulsa. The lift was being run by Sarah Page, a 17-year-old white girl. Not everything is clear about what happened in the lift, but most people agree that Rowland tripped and accidentally grabbed Page's arm. She screamed, and Rowland ran away, probably because he was afraid of what would happen if he was alone with a white woman who had just yelled. He was later arrested for allegedly hitting Page, but she didn't want to press charges.

The next day, the "Tulsa Tribune" ran a story about the lift incident that made it sound like Rowland tried to rape Page. This inflammatory news made things worse between different races in the city.

There were rumors that a white mob was going to kill Rowland when word got out that he had been arrested. As a result, groups of Black people, including some veterans of World War I, met at the courts to defend Rowland.

Tensions got out of hand when a group of white residents went to the jail to talk to the black residents. Several people were killed when shots were fired during a fight.

### The Horrifying Nights

Many white Tulsans were jealous of Greenwood's success in business, which made them feel bad about themselves. The end of Black Wall Street also meant the end of competition in the economy.

The fight at the courts was the start of a bigger spread of violence. White gangs started to steal from and burn down the Black neighborhood of Greenwood, which was called "Black Wall Street" because it was so wealthy. In 18 hours, the mobs burned 35 square blocks of Greenwood, killed up to 300 Black people, and forced thousands to leave their homes.

Nearly 1,200 homes caught fire as fires danced in the sky. These weren't just any houses; they were the result of Black families' hopes and hard work. Businesses, churches, schools, and even a hospital, all of which were owned and cared for by Black people, as well as homes, were destroyed by the fire. Some witnesses, whose voices were shaky but still strong, said that planes had fired on them from above, making things even worse on the ground.

For 48 scary hours, Greenwood went from a nice neighborhood to a place no one could even recognize. But the damage wasn't just to buildings. As the smoke cleared, stories came out about hundreds of people being led to camps at gunpoint, like animals. For weeks, they were locked up in these camps and couldn't get out until a white citizen vouched for them. Whispers rang off the walls of these camps. People talked about being forced to work without pay and about bodies being thrown into the Arkansas River or quickly buried in mass graves.

Even when the fires went out, those nights were still terrible. In the days that followed, Black residents were not comforted. Instead, they were rounded up and held at different makeshift holding centers, including the Convention Hall. Greenwood was troubled by what the city did for many years.

After almost 100 years, the ghosts of the past started to move around again. The search for the mass graves began in 2019, and by October 2020, a horrifying find was made in Oaklawn Cemetery. But the city wasn't done digging. On June 1, they planned to dig deeper, trying to close a terribly open chapter in history.

The survivors of the killing didn't get any compensation and no justice for the violence. The killing was mostly left out of history books, and people in Tulsa didn't talk about it publicly until many years later.

Recent efforts, especially around the 100th anniversary of the killing, have been aimed at making more people aware of this sad time in American history and how it still affects the Black community in Tulsa.

## *A Call for Justice: Three Voices from Tulsa*

On May 19, 2021, before the 100th anniversary of the Tulsa Race Massacre, Viola Fletcher appeared before the House Judiciary Subcommittee on the Constitution, Civil Rights, and Civil Liberties.

Three survivors stood tall in a room filled with echoes of the past. They were all tied together by memories of a nightmare that had changed their lives forever. Fletcher, Hughes "Uncle Red" Van Ellis, and Lessie Benningfield Randle were their names. They are 107, 100, and 106 years old, in that order. Each year wasn't just a sign of their age; it was also proof that they had lived through one of the worst times in American history.

Viola Fletcher looked every bit as strong as she was at 107 years old. She had silver hair and a strong will. Just two weeks before then, she had been enjoying another year of life with family and the hum of happy memories. Still, she was standing in the broad middle of Washington, D.C., for the first time. Not on vacation or for fun, but to demand justice, and make sure the rest of the country remembered the fires and violence in Tulsa in 1921.

She wasn't the only one. "Uncle Red" and Lessie, who stood next to her, each had their own troubling memories. Together, the three of them were more than just survivors; they were also fighters who led a court charge as the main claimants in a case to get compensation. A case that held the state of Oklahoma, the city of Tulsa, and other groups responsible for the terrible events that killed up to 300 Black people, made 10,000 people homeless and destroyed the thriving all-Black neighborhood of Greenwood.

## The Heartfelt Reminiscence

Fletcher told her story while wearing a mint-colored jacket that seemed to match her fresh and strong spirit. Even though she was old, her voice was clear and steady. It painted a picture of the past as the 100th anniversary of the killing got closer. With every word, she and her friends made one thing very clear: they would not be stopped in their drive for justice, respect, and restitution.

As Viola Fletcher started to tell her story from a hundred years ago, the room was quiet and there was a lot of tension in the air. It wasn't just a story; it took her back to a night that changed her life forever.

She talked about the night of May 31, 2021, when she fell asleep in her beloved Greenwood house. Greenwood was a symbol of wealth, culture, and history. There, young Viola was surrounded by laughter and love. She had a beautiful house, nice neighbors, and a group of playmates whose giggles were the essence of her youth. She had everything a child could want to feel safe and protected, and she had hopes for the future.

But that safety was gone in just a few hours. When the night's cover was pulled back, a scary dream was revealed. A group of angry white people had swarmed through Greenwood and caused a lot of damage. She was sleeping peacefully at home when her family woke her up and turned her world upside down. As they ran away, the frightening pictures of the violent mob burned into her young mind.

Viola said that the sounds from that night still come back to her in her dreams. Even though it's been a hundred years, the pain and suffering are still very real. Nations may choose to forget these dark times, but those who lived through them and their offspring still have the scars that tell the story. Their memories are live-proof, constant reminders of how terrible that night was.

As her voice faded, the room, which was full of members of Congress and other people, fell into a deep quiet. This silence was broken by the deep respect and sensitivity that her words had brought out in people. Then, like a wave, they stood up and gave Viola Fletcher the standing applause she so rightly deserved.

Hughes "Uncle Red" Van Ellis, who was 100 years old and had served in World War II, waited a moment before speaking. The room wasn't very bright. His eyes filled with tears, and the depths of them held a lot of different feelings, like pride, pain, and betrayal. He was happy to wear the uniform and serve his country abroad, but the country he fought for denied him justice. He begged with a shaking voice, "Don't let me leave this world without justice like so many others have."

As a leader in the fight for racial justice, Dreisen Heath pointed out the terrible irony. While Tulsa and Oklahoma watched their survivors die off, they refused to admit their guilt or make up for what they had done. Justice has been hard to find for almost a hundred years. Heath asked the House Judiciary Subcommittee on the Constitution, Civil Rights, and Civil Liberties to listen, recognize, and take action while the last people who saw the horrors of Greenwood were still alive.

Heath's voice shook with emotion as he thought about all the dead people who had waited in vain for justice. Viola Fletcher was one of them. She told stories about her life, which was full of lies and betrayals.

In that room, history wasn't just lines on a page; it was a live, breathing testament to a community's strength and a constant call for respect and justice.

## 4. VIOLA FLETCHER'S VOICE: A SOUND HOPE

The way Viola Fletcher has lived her life shows how strong the human spirit is. She has been alive for an amazing 109 years and has seen some of the most important events in history. Through the changing sands of time, she has seen nations rise and fall, the wonders of human creativity, and both the saddest and greatest parts of the 20th and 21st centuries.

At her age, Fletcher has memories of a time and place that most of us can only make up. She lived through the ups and downs of the 20th century, from the terrible World Wars that changed world politics to the scientific breakthroughs that have made modern life what it is today. She lived through the spread of diseases like polio and H1N1, the fear of storms, the terrible dust bowl droughts, and pandemics like the Spanish Flu in 1918 and Covid-19, which happened recently. She also lived through the Great Depression, a time when the economy was terrible.

In all of the above, the horrible events of the Tulsa Race Massacre on Black Wall Street were what left a lasting mark on Fletcher's mind. This wasn't just another historical event she read about or saw on TV... People of color have had to deal with prejudice and institutional racism for generations, and the damage and deaths that day are a clear reminder of that.

But her view isn't just about the bad things that happen. She has been amazed by people's desire to study the stars, seen the birth of molecular medicine, and seen how green energy sources are used. There have been times of awe and wonder for every time of pain and loss.

Her understanding of how complicated people are is very deep. She has met people from all walks of life, from the bad to the good, from world leaders to everyday heroes. She has learned from interacting with them that terms like wealthy, educated, or poor don't say anything about a person's worth or humanity. They just tell you where they stand in society.

Fletcher's impact talks about how important understanding is with the kind of knowledge that only comes with age. Her message is mostly about recognizing pain and wrongdoings from the past and making a promise to make sure they don't happen again. She thinks that even though everyone has different goals, interests, and wants, health is something that everyone values. It's the golden thread that ties us all together and the key to a rich and full life.

It's a rare treat to meet someone like Fletcher. She is a live piece of history, connecting the past and the present. Through her eyes, we can see a hundred years of struggles, dreams, and changes. Above all, her life shows that ideas like justice and equality might be hard to grasp, but that we can bring them to life by working together.

Her life story has come to see life as a fabric made of many different events. Some of the lines are the teachers whose knowledge has left a permanent mark, while others are the caregivers whose acts of kindness light the way forward. No matter who you are or what you've been through, there are times when you feel like you're on the edge and need someone to pull you back. When things are tough, we can get through them with the help of our mental toughness, physical health, and the support networks we've built up.

But being strong isn't the only thing that makes someone resilient. It's also about recognizing the many sides of other people and realizing that everyone has their own experiences and points of view. We shouldn't get stuck in the mud of past deaths or problems. Instead, we should use those things as stepping stones and learn from them so that we can reach higher heights.

She has been a good observer for many years, which has given her a deep understanding of life's subtleties. Instead of rushing into the future with all of our hopes and dreams, maybe we could look around, and enjoy the little things. After all, it's often these small, seemingly unimportant things that make up the bigger picture of our lives.

No matter where we come from or what our life stories are, there are some things that never change. The desire for safety and a place to hide from the storms of life; the need for clean air, water, and food to stay alive; and the natural desire to learn, love, and be loved in return. These are not just wants; they are basic rights. And every person, no matter where they come from, deserves these rights and the respect that keeps them in place.

Indeed, Viola Fletcher's life and words show a timeless truth: that we can create a more caring and inclusive world by understanding and accepting our shared humanity.

## 5. THE VIOLA FORD FLETCHER FOUNDATION

The waves of time often erase memories, water down ideas, and even change people's beliefs. Yet, in the middle of this huge desert of time, Viola Fletcher stands as a symbol of leadership, and vision. She is not just a witness to history; instead, she is an example of a powerful force that changes the future.

Fletcher thinks that being a leader is a complicated dance of knowledge, insight, and kindness. It's not just about having names or getting people to do what you say. It means recognizing how closely the lives of all people are connected and making music out of the sounds of separation. As the world struggles with labels that divide people and differences that seem impossible to bridge, Viola's mindset gives people hope. She believes in care, not dominance. She believes in making roads, not putting up walls. She believes in lighting the way, not just leading.

The Viola Ford Fletcher Foundation (VFFF) shows this idea in a beautiful way. Here, the goal is clear: to break the chains of unfairness and lack of power through education, health care, and opportunities. It's also about teaching them to be self-reliant, feeding their desire, and making sure everyone has the tools they need to shape their own lives.

The fact that Viola survived the horrible Tulsa Race Massacre and then went on to become the genius behind VFFF shows how strong and determined she is. It shows how much she believes that humanity can rise, rebuild, and thrive even in the face of unimaginable hardship.

The foundation stresses that group growth is more important than individual success.

Through its many projects and partnerships, VFFF is creating a place where trust is the standard, not the exception.

Leaders like Viola Fletcher tell us that we all have the same hopes and goals and that our lives are tied together. Viola Fletcher sends a powerful message through her foundation and unbreakable spirit: The future is collaboration, open to everyone, and full of promise if we are brave enough to put aside our differences and move forward together.

According to what Fletcher stated in her letter to the leaders of humanity, people are fundamentally the same. They require access to clean water, air, and food, as well as safe areas that are free from violence where they may lay their heads, raise children, learn, love, and be loved while also being respected. She went on to say that she believes people have a strong desire to be a part of their communities because those communities encourage and enable individuals to discover their full potential. Fletcher is of the opinion that if a person's fundamental requirements are addressed, they are in a position where they are more open to learning and dreaming.

Fletcher has expressed the hope that the Viola Ford Fletcher Foundation will serve as a means by which individuals might move from the realm of possibility into one that is more justifiable and equitable. She also desires for the foundation to serve as a forum in which those with the highest levels of expertise could collaborate with one another in an organizational setting that is open to new forms of information and technology with the goal of bettering people's lives as well as the life of the planet. People's ways of doing things form a framework for them to do the right things, for the right reasons, since they are concerned about and value their own ability to survive and continue existing. Fletcher wanted to make possibilities that gave people renewed hope and increased stress levels. She had a fantasy of bringing everyone to the same level by disseminating information that was very important, delivering it to those who were in need of it, and assisting those individuals in becoming healthy and independent.

Fletcher has entrusted her grandson with the responsibility of realizing these goals before she kicks the bucket. As a result, she appealed to everyone to support her grandson's efforts to assist people in becoming healthy, affluent, and wise since she believed that no child should have to go through pain.

# 6. VIOLA AND HUMANITY

## VFFF Ghana

As the first month of 2023 began in Ghana, the local chapter of The Viola Ford Fletcher Foundation brought a wave of love and happiness to the crowd. The 14th of January was not just another day; it was a sign of hope for the people at Osu Children's Home, New Horizon Special School, and Dzorwulu Special School.

The generosity of Shoprite, Indomie Ghana, and Le Country Water, which sponsored the party, made the air full of thanks and music. Even though it was a small act, it summed up what the VFFF is all about helping those who are less fortunate by shining a light into their lives and lifting their moods.

The event took place at the New Horizon Special School in Cantonment, Accra. The happy steps of young dancers on the dance floor told stories of strength and happiness that touched everyone there. Kids and their teachers played fun games like dance-offs and musical chairs, which made everyone laugh and cheer.

Rev. Tony White, who is in charge of operations at the foundation, was the first person to speak. With a kind heart, he explained what the day was all about and how the foundation has always wanted to bring a little happiness and food into the lives of these loved ones.

But the feeling did not end there. The Vice President of the Foundation, His Royal Majesty Eze Dr. Amb Chukwudi Ihenetu, who is also the respected Paramount King of the Igbo People in Ghana, sat with the special children and promised to keep working together. With knowledge and kindness, he told the young people to hold on to their faith and told them that things would get better with God's help. Above all, he stressed that their "special" label wasn't just a name. It was proof that they deserved a lot of extra love and care. His passionate plea was for everyone to work together to help these young stars and make sure they got the care they earned. Throughout, he thanked the school's hardworking staff from the bottom of his heart and praised their endless love and dedication.

Then, Madam Mariama Obeng, who is the Deputy Principal of New Horizon Special School's trade center, spoke. While her words were full of thanks for the foundation's kindness, there was also a soft request that reminded me of the story of Oliver Twist. A call for more, not out of greed but because we need it. Even though their hearts were full, their daily operations often put a strain on their funds. She talked about how hard it was to take care of the needs of these special people and asked donors to help so that no child's needs went unmet.

## About the Dzorwulu Special School

The Dzorwulu Special School is a well-known government-run school that is known for helping children with autism.

The idea for this place came from a deep worry about how hard it was for many parents to raise their autistic children on their own, which was made worse by the shame that society has against autistic people. The school is meant to be a safe place for these kids. It gives them care, and education, and helps them find their secret talents.

Two caring people, Mrs. Josephine Afrifa, a dedicated social worker, and Mr. E. S. Aidoo, a recognized Judicial Secretary at the time, had the idea for this kind of safe place. Together, they started the "Society of Friends of Mentally Challenged Children" because they cared a lot about kids with autism. At first, these children stayed at the Accra Psychiatric Hospital with adult patients. But because society wanted to improve the lives of these children even more, they saw the need for a recovery and care center with skill training.

At the end of 1970, thanks to a successful fundraising effort, the society was able to lay the groundwork for a school that would care for children. The center did well because the government helped by making sure that educational, household, and medical needs were met through the Ministries of Education and Health. And in 1974, the society handed over control to the government in a smooth way. This is how the famous Dzorwulu Special School we know today came to be.

In 1949, a group of Ghanaian women and a Norwegian woman set up the school as a Child Care Society. Their goal was to care for orphans and other children in need. The government of Ghana at the time took over the society in 1962, and it was then put under the control of the Department of

Social Welfare. After that, it was moved to where it is now, in Labone, and given a new name: Osu Children's Home. Its goal is to care for and protect children who are morally or physically in danger. The Ministry of Gender, Children, and Social Protection, which is in charge of the Department of Social Welfare at the moment, is in charge of the home.

In 1949, a group of forward-thinking Ghanaian women and a caring Norwegian woman came together to start a good cause.

## About The New Horizon Special School

In 1972, Mrs. Salome Francois established the institution that would become the school. It offers day school education to children between the ages of 6 and 18, as well as vocational training and employment opportunities to persons with intellectual disabilities who are 18 years of age or older. In addition to providing children and people with special needs with a complete education in a setting that is both safe and nurturing, their goal is to cultivate each child's potential to its fullest so that he or she can live a life that is both fruitful and satisfying. If a person's principal handicap is a learning challenge, then they may be admitted even if they have additional disabilities as well. Some examples of these additional disabilities are spasticity, cerebral palsy, vision impairment, hearing impairment, and so on. Bead making, kente weaving, batik dying, and basket weaving are just a few of the vocational activities that they offer. Life skills such as ironing, cleaning, and basic cooking are taught to older children as part of an effort to prepare them for independent living.

## About the Osu Children's Home

In the middle of 1949, a group of innovative Ghanaian women and a caring Norwegian woman came together to start a good cause. Their hope? To make a safe place for orphans and other fragile children, called the Child Care Society, where they can feel safe and loved. Still, as the winds of time blew, this symbol of hope was given to the Ghanaian government in 1962. With this change, the home moved to Labone and got a new name: the Osu Children's Home. Its new goal was not just to care for its young inmates, but also to protect them from moral and physical dangers. Today, the Department of Social Welfare, which is run by the Ministry of Gender, Children, and Social Protection, keeps an eye on this safe place.

# 7. FINAL THOUGHT

Every once in a while, in the pages of history, a name comes up that defies the passage of time and stands as a testament to strength, vision, and hope. Viola Fletcher is definitely one of these important people.

At the heart of many important projects that change things for the better is the strong spirit of a single person. Viola Fletcher comes across as such an unstoppable force as we read through these pages. She is a shining example of strength, hope, and a clear vision that never changes. Her life, which has been shaped by a lot of different things she's done and how determined she's been, becomes the symbol of a dream she passes on to her beloved grandson.

Viola's goals weren't just about what she wanted for herself. Instead, she fought for a cause that was important to a lot of people. She was a strong believer that every child, no matter what their background was, could hope for a healthy, wealthy, and wise life. This is based on her strong opinion that no child should ever have to go through pain or lack and that the young should never have to deal with these things.

While most people are happy to just hope, Viola is a woman who took action. The Viola Ford Fletcher Foundation was made because of her drive. It was not only a sign of how much she cared, but it also became a live, breathing representation of what she wanted. As we learned about the foundation's many projects, it became clear that it only had one goal: to bring light into the lives of people who were in the dark because of problems, lift their spirits, and pave the way for better days to come.

Rev. Tony White's heartfelt words, His Royal Majesty Eze Dr. Amb Chukwudi Ihenetu's deep promises, and Madam Mariama Obeng's emotional requests—all of these voices came together to echo Viola's hopes. Not only were these people people, but they also became guardians of her vision and keepers of her heritage.

But as the story went on, it became clear that this trip was not without problems. Each step forward was met with its own set of problems, which showed how hard the foundation had to work to overcome stereotypes, and most importantly, false beliefs about the people it was trying to help.

When we think about Viola Fletcher's life and impact, her story is very personal, it goes beyond her own life. It urges each of us to look beyond ourselves and imagine a world where kindness is the most important thing, where every child is respected, and where dreams, no matter how crazy, can make things happen.

Names come and go in the history books, but Viola Fletcher's will always be there, not just as a person, but also as a sign of hope, determination, and love that knows no bounds. Her memory pushes us all to think, to act, and, to believe that good change is not only possible but also within our reach.

Made in the USA
Monee, IL
26 May 2025